Coral Reef

Written by Steve Parker
Edited by Natalie Boyd and Sarah Powell
Designed by Simon Webb and Nicola Friggens

priddy books
big ideas for little people

All about coral

Corals are special rocks found in the sea. They have amazing shapes — and they grow! Corals are made by tiny creatures called coral polyps. They can look like tables, mushrooms, vases, chimneys, trees, and many other shapes. Some are smaller than your hand, while others are bigger than a house!

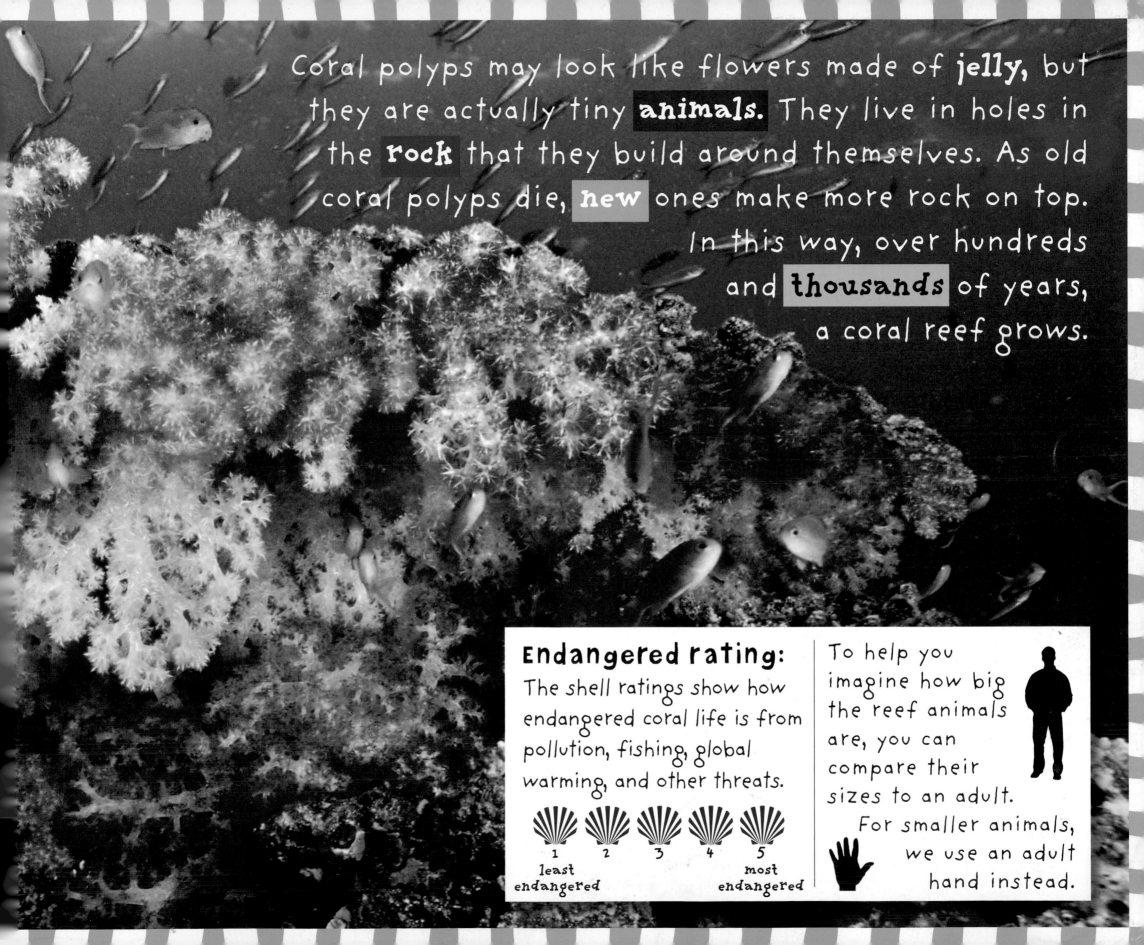

Coral polyps may look like flowers made of **jelly**, but they are actually tiny **animals.** They live in holes in the **rock** that they build around themselves. As old coral polyps die, **new** ones make more rock on top. In this way, over hundreds and **thousands** of years, a coral reef grows.

Endangered rating:

The shell ratings show how endangered coral life is from pollution, fishing, global warming, and other threats.

1	2	3	4	5
least endangered				most endangered

To help you imagine how big the reef animals are, you can compare their sizes to an adult. For smaller animals, we use an adult hand instead.

Reefs of the world

Names of the reefs

1: Caribbean reefs
2: West Atlantic Seaboard reefs
3: North Atlantic cold-water reefs
4: Mid Atlantic reefs
5: Red Sea reefs
6: Gulf reefs
7: Indian Ocean reefs
8: Maldives reefs
9: Sunda reefs
10: South China Sea reefs
11: Celebes reefs
12: Great Barrier Reef
13: Coral Sea reefs
14: Pacific Island reefs
15: New Zealand cold-water reefs

North America

South America

Some corals grow in cold water, such as the shores of the Atlantic Ocean in the USA and Europe

Corals grow mainly around oceans in the middle of the world, such as the **Tropics**. Here the water is warm, **shallow,** and clear. They form huge **groups** of rocks called **coral reefs.**

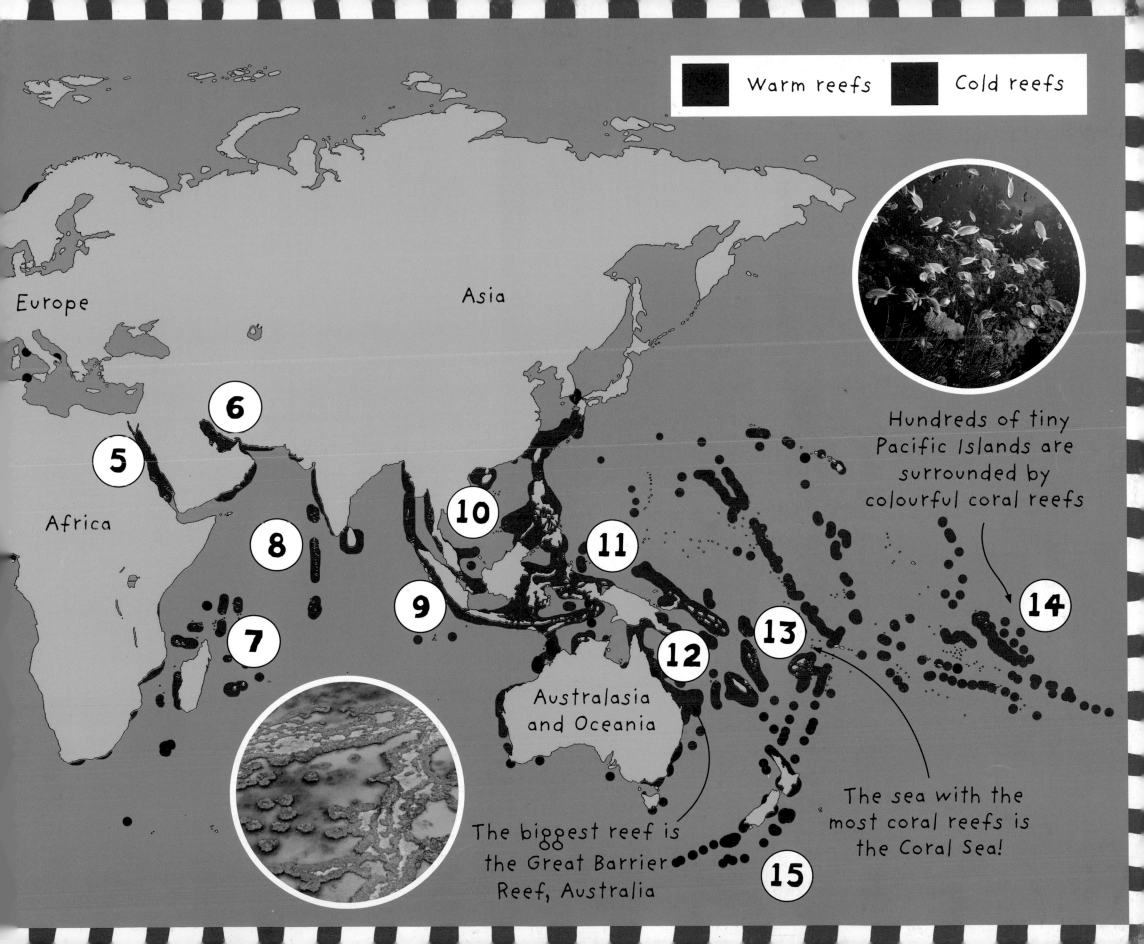

Warm reefs   Cold reefs

Europe

Asia

Africa

Australasia
and Oceania

5
6
7
8
9
10
11
12
13
14
15

Hundreds of tiny
Pacific Islands are
surrounded by
colourful coral reefs

The biggest reef is
the Great Barrier
Reef, Australia

The sea with the
most coral reefs is
the Coral Sea!

Coral polyps

Polyps, like their cousins the jellyfish and sea anemones, are **killers!** They sting and then swallow their tiny victims, bringing them into their mouths, which are in the middle of their **tentacles.** Polyps have tiny **plants** called algae that live in their bodies and that they also **share** food with. Polyps feed at night, and the reef shines with brilliant **colours.**

Polyps branch like mini-trees

Fun fact
Some groups of deep-sea coral polyps are more than 4,000 years old!

Fact file

Size, most less than:
1 in (2.5 cm) tall

Lives:
Warm clear shallow seas

Endangered rating:

One of the greatest ocean **wanderers** is the green turtle. It can swim more than 2,000 miles (3,200 km) each year. It is **protected** by a huge, thick **shell,** and its paddle-shaped front flippers row powerfully through the water.

While active, turtles must **breathe** air every few minutes or they will drown.

Fun fact
A sleeping turtle can stay underwater for six hours!

Sharp-edged "beak" snips plant food

Fact file

Size up to:
5 ft (1.5 m)

Lives:
Warm oceans and seas

Endangered rating:

Green turtle

Moray eel

Mouth can open very wide

Fun fact
The moray has very sharp teeth in its jaws — and in its throat, too!

Hiding in its rocky **cave** or cracks among the coral, the laced moray **watches** and waits for fish and other prey. Then, quick as a **flash**, it stretches out its long snake-like body and **grabs** its meal with sharp teeth, before **squirming** back into its den to swallow its **feast**.

Fact file

Size up to:
10 ft (3 m) long

Lives: Indian Ocean and Pacific Ocean

Endangered rating:

The rusty parrotfish has its **upper** and lower **teeth** packed closely together, forming a hard, strong **"beak."** This scrapes and **scratches** the rocks and reefs to take in all kinds of small animals and plants. The swallowed **rock** breaks down inside the fish and comes out as tiny white **grains** – coral sand!

Hard scales

Fact file

Size up to:
16 in (40 cm)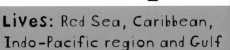

Lives: Red Sea, Caribbean, Indo-Pacific region and Gulf

Endangered rating:

Parrotfish

There are more than 60 kinds of snakes that live in the sea. The banded sea snake can hold its breath for **two hours** and dive down more than 200 ft (60 m)! Its fangs inject powerful **venom** into eels and other fish. It must leave the water and come onto land to change its skin and lay eggs.

Long, bendy body

Fun fact

This sea snake swims into rivers, wriggles onto land, and can even climb trees!

Sea snake

Slugs on land are dull-looking, but not in the sea! The lettuce sea slug **slides** along on its **slimy** foot, its frilly back shining with amazing **colours**. This bright display **warns** other creatures that a sea slug tastes horrible and may even **poison** them, so they leave it alone!

Sea slug

Fun fact
The lettuce sea slug lays up to 500 eggs at one time!

Fact file

Size up to:
2 in (5 cm)

Lives:
Caribbean and West Atlantic

Endangered rating:

Tentacles at head end

By far the world's **biggest** coral reef, the Great Barrier Reef stretches along **Australia's** northeast shore. This vast chain of almost **3,000** separate reefs and nearly 1,000 islands has over 1,500 kinds of fish, **5,000** types of shellfish, 200 kinds of seabirds, and 50 different types of shark!

Fun fact
One of the world's biggest creatures visits the reef — the 36,000 kg humpback whale.

Heart Reef's rocky coral outcrops naturally form a heart shape

Fact file
Size: More than 1,600 miles (2,575 km) long

Variety: More than 400 kinds of corals

Age: Most areas are less than 10,000 years old

Great Barrier Reef

Cleaner shrimp

Tiny pincers pick up small bits of food

Fun fact
A fish waiting to be cleaned opens its mouth wide, showing it's safe for the shrimp to enter.

The scarlet cleaner shrimp waits on its **favourite** rock for a "customer" to **clean.** This is usually a fish that has tiny pests, such as fish lice, on its skin, gills, and even inside its **mouth.** The cleaner shrimp crawls over the **customer,** picking off the **pests** and eating them! The shrimp gets a meal and the fish gets clean and healthy.

Fact file

Size up to:
2 in (5 cm)

Lives: Mediterranean and Red Sea

Endangered rating:

The **leafy** sea dragon, a relation of the sea horse, has fins, fronds, and fleshy folds that make it look like a piece of **seaweed**. Its appearance makes it difficult for its **enemies** to spot it, and it's one of nature's best examples of **camouflage** – looking like your surroundings.

Fins waft back and forth in currents, like seaweed

Fact file

Size up to:
14 in (35 cm)

Lives: Indian Ocean and Australian coast

Endangered rating:

Fun fact
The sea dragon is one of the world's slowest-swimming fish!

Sea dragon

The lionfish looks so **beautiful** with its long, **stripy,** wavy fin spines. But these spines can jab in a **venom** that is deadly to many other sea creatures, though rarely to people. This fish is a very skilled **predator,** able to swallow **prey** whole in one single super-fast gulp.

Fun fact
A lionfish's stomach can expand to 30 times its normal size.

Fin spines have sharp tips

Fact file

Size up to:
17 in (43 cm)

Lives: Indo-Pacific Oceans, Western Atlantic and Caribbean

Endangered rating:

Lionfish

Fact file

Head to tail:
5 ft (1.5 m)

Lives: Indian Ocean and Western Pacific Ocean

Endangered rating:

Beware of the **blue-spotted** stingray! On the underside of its tail base are two hard, sharp stingers. Like small knives, these **inject** a very painful venom. This ray **glides** slowly over the flat areas between coral rocks, looking for worms, crabs, and similar creatures **hiding** under the sand.

Pectoral fins like wings

Stingray

Fun fact
Hammerhead sharks will eat stingrays — they don't care about the stings!

The red pencil urchin hides by day and comes out at **night** to feed. Its **mouth** on its underside scrapes rocks for food and its long blunt spines wave back and forth as **protection**. Urchins move using long, **bendy** parts called "tube feet," which poke out of the ball-shaped **shell**.

Fun fact
An urchin's mouth has five sharp teeth in a ring, and can chew through stone!

Fact file

Size up to: 10 in (25 cm) across

Lives: Pacific Islands, especially Hawaii

Endangered rating:

Sea urchin

Reef shark

Fun fact

Female blacktip reef sharks give birth to babies as small as 12 in (30 cm) long.

All fins have black tips

Mouth on underside of head

The blacktip reef shark swims around its home reef, **watching** and smelling, ready to race after prey ... then **snap!** It eats mainly **fish,** but also gulps down shrimp, prawns, crabs, worms, **sea snakes,** squid, octopus, baby turtles, seabirds ... almost anything!

Fact file

Size up to: 6 ft (1.8 m) long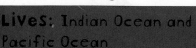

Lives: Indian Ocean and Pacific Ocean

Endangered rating:

The world's **biggest** shellfish, the giant clam, weighs as much as four adult humans. It sucks in water to **filter** out tiny floating animals and **plants** as food. Also, like coral polyps, the clam has micro-plants in its **body,** which share their food with the clam. In return the clam gives them a **safe** place to live.

Fun fact
Once settled in a reef, giant clams stay there for life, which can be over 100 years!

Fact file

Size up to: 4 ft (1.2 m) across

Lives: South East Asia and Pacific Ocean

Endangered rating:

Giant clam

This is one of the biggest, most **harmful**, and hungriest **starfish** in the world! It has more than 20 arms and its spines inject a **venom** that causes **stinging** pain and bleeding. Crown of thorns eat coral polyps and other small reef creatures, causing huge **damage** to reefs.
It's an all round bad guy!

Each arm has over 50 spines

Crown of thorns

Fact file

Size up to: 28 in (70 cm) across

Lives: Indian Ocean and Pacific Ocean

Endangered rating:

Triggerfish

Fact file

Size up to: 20 in (50 cm) long

Lives: Indian Ocean and Pacific Ocean

Endangered rating:

First dorsal fin has stiff spine at front

The clown triggerfish has **hard** teeth that form a **"beak"** for scraping up and **cracking** open food. These fish also have a "trigger," a spine that lies flat on its back. This "trigger" can tilt to **stab** at an enemy, or **wedge** the fish into a crack so it cannot be pulled out.

Fun fact
This fish's teeth are so strong, it can easily crack open a crab's shell!

There are more than **200** coral reefs in the **Caribbean** region, with about 600 kinds of fish. They form nearly 10 percent of the **world's** coral reef areas. However, its coral shapes are often smashed by huge **storms** called **hurricanes** from June to November every year.

Lots of sea life is found here, such as Sergeant Major fish

Caribbean reefs

Fun fact
Reefs have grown on many Caribbean shipwrecks, including pirate ones!

After hiding by day in its cave, or lair, the Caribbean reef octopus comes out at night to hunt. It has eight long, bendy arms with suckers to catch prey such as crabs, shrimps, lobsters, and fish. The octopus tears up the victim with its parrot-like beak which is positioned in the middle of its arms.

Its main body looks like a bag

Fun fact
The reef octopus can change colour, such as from red to green, in just a few seconds!

Reef octopus

Sea anemones are animals with no eyes, ears, heart, or **brain**. However, they are deadly predators, catching and **stinging** victims with their tentacles, before **swallowing** them into their mouths. Anemones have many different bright **colours**, from pink and yellow, to blue, green, purple, and black.

Fun fact

Some types of sea anemones can live up to 80 years!

Fact file

Size: Mostly 1 to 4 in (2.5 to 10 cm) tall

Lives: Most oceans and seas

Endangered rating:

Sea anemone

Clownfish

The clownfish loves to stay safe among the tentacles of its **anemone** "friend." Its thin covering of **slime** stops the sea anemone's stings — the same stings that keep **predators** away. In return, the clownfish eats bits of leftover food among the **tentacles,** keeping the sea anemone **clean.**

Large pectoral (side) fins for swimming

Fact file

Size up to: 4 in (10 cm) long

Lives: Eastern Indian Ocean and Western Pacific Ocean

Endangered rating:

Reefs at risk

Coral reefs are full of beautiful **wildlife.** Few other places have so many kinds of animals and plants. But all around the world, reefs are in **danger.**

As global warming affects the oceans, the rising water temperature **kills** the coral polyps. The reefs look pale and lifeless; this is known as **"bleaching."**

River **pollution** causes more soil and mud to travel from the **land,** making the water cloudy. This covers the coral polyps, smothering them to death.

People catch sea creatures in many **damaging** ways. They drag **nets** along the ocean floor, pour poison into the water, and even set off **dynamite!**

Glossary

Algae Types of simple plants that mostly live in the sea, from microscopic blob-like algae that float in the water or live inside some animals' bodies, up to huge seaweeds many metres long.

Bleaching To make white or very pale in colour.

Camouflage Use of shapes, colours, patterns, and movements to look like the surroundings and blend in, so as not to be noticed.

Coral Coral polyps and the rocks they make.

Dorsal A structure that grows from the back or upper surface of an animal.

Endangered At risk of disappearing or dying out.

Fangs Long, thin teeth suited for jabbing and stabbing.

Fins Wide, flap-like body parts that help with movement, as on a fish or dolphin.

Fronds Wavy-edged, floppy, leaf-like parts on a plant such as a seaweed, or on some animals such as sea dragons.

Gills Feathery body parts that underwater animals use for "breathing," to take in oxygen from water.

Global warming Rise in temperature of the whole Earth, including its seas and oceans, due to the activities of people, especially burning fuels such as petrol, diesel, coal, oil, and natural gas.

Hurricane A huge storm with very strong winds, which occurs from June to November in the Caribbean.

Microplants Tiny plants that are so small they can only be seen through a microscope.

Poison A dangerous substance produced by some animals that can cause great pain